Some Reflections

Matthew Nesbitt

Presentation by *BookLeaf Publishing*

Web: www.bookleafpub.com

E-mail: info@bookleafpub.com

ISBN: 9789357615594

First edition 2022

Recorder of Deeds

Satisfactions,
Mortgages, Deeds, and
Other documents

To record in packs
Of one, two, three, or more. Not
By hand but by computer

Phones ring and we
Answer the publics' questions,
Many ways to say the same thing

Documents come in
Different ways-by mail, by
Runners, by third party

If the document
Does not fit our criteria
It is rejected-

Returned to sender
With a note-with directions
How to fit it.

Special Education

A branch of teaching a person is called towards
These teachers may not be nominated for
different awards
Working with students who have different
educational needs

Tough but rewarding, some providing itinerant
levels of support
Meeting with their students for a little awhile,
keeping the time short.
Others are stationed in a classroom within the
school

Some teach life skills, others learning support,
others are more specific
Working in emotional support or with students
who are autistic
As well as teachers who work with students who
are medically fragile

Working with the gifted students also falls into
special education
People do not think of it as that since they are
beyond intelligent in their formation

Way above average yet still possess its own
challenges

It is its own community, with benefits and
challenges
Overwhelming but has checks and balances
Most teachers struggle to adapt their style
because they do not want to change

A branch of teaching a person is called towards
These teachers may not be nominated for
different awards
Working with students who have different
educational needs

Autistic Support

Teaching skills that come naturally to others but at a slower pace,
Breaking them down into smaller steps for them to master,
Skills like tying their shoes, buttoning their coat, or washing their hands and face

Some of them can only say a few words or have a few phrases that are on repeat
Others will be nonverbal, unable to talk but using sign language or a device to communicate
Others will be able to speak in sentences complete

To learn new vocabulary and to practice motor skills
Intensive teaching sessions are done throughout the day
Repetition is key but cannot lack any of the thrills

"What is this?" "Do this" Show me"…the phrases to use go on and on
A ratio between tasks and favorite things varies per student

You have to keep it fast pace-then the student
will not yawn

Each one has a different deck of cards
Pictures of items to label and actions to imitate
Ranging in difficulty from easy to hard.

Patience is the name of the game. It may take a
while to learn a basic skill
It is one step towards independence
When it happens, we are overjoyed and are
thrilled.

Emotional Support

Working with students who look no different
from any other
Until a line, seen or unseen, is crossed-Then run
for cover

Some will go from one to ten, skipping the
numbers in-between
Summoning great strength from a frame so lean

Controlling emotions comes with great difficulty
Something that is learned intentionally instead
of just coming naturally

Teaching social skills, academics, and how to
relate to the world around them
Their behavior can be difficult and there are
moments that feel like mayhem

There are times when there is calm after the
storm
Moments that can make your heart feel warm

There are aspects of the students' life that are
out of our control
But it is part of our job to provide a positive role

It is tough at times to work with them for
particular reasons
They will test our patience and the classroom's
cohesion

They will challenge our authority and intentions
We need to be humble and be willing to provide
suggestions

Every day is a new day, to try again
But all of our attempts are not in vain

We can't save them all but we can give them all
a chance
Remembering that they are here because of
particular circumstance.

Warehouse

Welcome to work's first day
Ready for long hours for decent pay
Eight-to-twelve-hour shifts-four to six days a week
At first your muscle will ache, and your bones feel like they will creak

Each department has its own function like a part of the human body
Or a complex machine that can be efficient or spotty.
Receiving brings merchandise in to be defused throughout the complex
To be stored for later harvest by the Pickers, collecting items for the customer's order with every step.
After the harvest is done and the totes are full, it is sent down the steel river to the Packers
Who separate and package the customer's orders before sending them to the department that matters.
Shipping loads the trucks and makes sure the orders at sent out on time,
Their part of the river is free from blockage that the customer's orders don't miss the deadline.

If the customer does not like their order, they
can send it back and Returns will handle it
Processing it and sending it back into the mix to
become another person's outfit.

Most employees are just a part of the machine,
not paid to think
Yet with a high turnover, a common site is
seeing department numbers shrink.
Despite that the machine marches on, expecting
the rest to make up for the fallen
Requiring mandatory overtime and working at
110 percent, going all in.
You are letting everyone down when you call
out sick
This can feel like a guilt trip even though they
have other tricks.
Making promises that we can or will not keep
Might be a way for an issue to be ignored or
swept
Under the rug, not to be addressed that will just
add to the mess
All of these factors add to the overall low morale
and stress
Your patience and endurance is put to the test
Some people can thrive in this environment but
for others, the fit is not the best.

Night at the Ballpark

Take me out to the ball game -
I need to be there early, before the gates open
after five.
The employees clock in and prepare for tonight's
special events,
The different promotions that are happening on
the field.
We all arrive at our stations before the gates
open.
The ticket takers are the first to meet the crowd.
The people who purchased tickets for the season
are the first to enter
Before the rest of the crowd.

Once inside, ushers show you to your seat.
If you are in need of food and drink- more
options than just peanuts and Cracker Jacks.
Hot dogs, hamburgers, pretzels, soda, beer, and
many other options await
At the cushions stand around the stadium or at
the Broken Bat
There are crowds of visitors-some for the first
time, some who come on occasion
There are the regulars who are at every game-the
stadium their second home

They don't care if they never get back
To their first home.

After the National Anthem is sung and everyone
is settled in,
"Play ball"- the game has begun.
Most of us root, root, root for the
Barnstormers-the home team.
Some have traveled to root for the visiting team.
After a while, it is time to stretch and take a
walk
A time to explore,
To see what else is going on at the ball game.

Visited the cushion stands for a refill and some
more food.
A playground and games over by the third base
side in left field
Lawn seating in the outfield, skybox seats above
the first level of seating
Found the Broken Bat beer deck-a seller of local
brews
A few feet away is a place you can get your
nicotine fix.

After the seventh inn stretch and singing "Take
me out to the Ballgame"
It is the bottom of the eighth and the score is
tied.

If the Barnstormers don't win, it's a shame.
After making a grand slam, they are up by four.

The top of the ninth, two outs and the tension is
high
The pitcher has been on fire, the crowd feeling
the energy.
Last player up to bat for the night, and we all
know the phrase
"For it's one, two, three strikes, you're out"
The crowd jumps and cheers "The Stormer's
won!"
What a game, what a close game.
As the crowd leaves, other staff members come
to clean up the mess left behind
It is only the start of the home stand.
Two more games like this one at the stadium.
What a night at the ballpark-at the old ball
game!

The Dutchman's Palace

On the highway controlled by Lincoln
Sits the palace and the castle of the Dutchman
Its walls make the entrance into a vast park
With his watchmen on guard day and night
A carnival all year round,
The merchants have games for the guests to play
And rides for them to enjoy
Many guests bring their children who have a
great time.
Vendors with different dishes are stationed
throughout the carnival
And minstrels perform over the course of the
day.
The carpenters and architects come out to check
on the rides of the carnival
To make sure everything is running smoothly.
The gardeners move throughout, cleaning up
after others and making sure
Everything is well stocked and cleaned.
They all work together to make sure their guests
have a grand time
And the children say "Let's go back to Dutch
Wonderland

Sunday School

Sunday morning comes around, ready for
Liturgy to begin
Understood the lesson that is to be taught today,
prepared what I will say
Naturally nervous during the service, I continued
to pray
Divine Liturgy is on its way, the Epistle and
Gospel readings
And the Anaphora is prayed along with Our
Father. Then Holy Communion
Younger grades are the first to receive before
their teachers and other students

Students settle into their seats before the lesson
begins
Class starts with a prayer. The teacher models
how to make the Sign of the Cross
"Holy God, Holy Mighty, Holy Immortal, have
mercy on us" the class prays together
On this Sunday, we talked about feelings and
how God cares about our feelings.
Our emotions are not "good" or "bad" by
themselves; it is how we express them
Lastly, we reviewed the lesson before Coffee
Hour.

Mission Trips

Raising money to travel
To another part of the country to help people in
need
And if they inquire first, share the Gospel

Going to Sutton to paint an elderly couple's
home the first year
The next year, traveling to Red Mesa
To paint a house in southern Utah for the Navajo

A new year, a new destination
To Middletown-to paint inside a woman's home
While others worked outside in the heat and
humidity

The last trip was to Port Jarvis
Helping to put a fresh coat of paint on the
outside of a local music shop.
I am grateful for these experiences

Small Town Library

A part of a large
Network of local libraries
Relies on volunteers

Checking in books that
Were dropped off the night before
Before putting them back

Using the Dewey
Decimal system to file
Each book to its spot

When a patron checks
Out a book, it is due back
In two weeks' time

When their card expires
We update it and can provide
A new one as needed.

Giving Your Time

Donations can come in many forms
Money the most common
But time is equally important

To help prepare meals for the homeless or for an
organization
Like Meals on Wheels or MANNA
Or at a soup kitchen.

Take the time to help someone who is struggling
with a subject
Volunteer to teach Sunday school

Help someone move, paint their home, or
redecorate
Spend some time helping those in need
There are many ways to give your time

Time

An invisible force that surrounds us all
That was created and has its own law
It does not have a constant speed
It moves like a snail or like a cheetah that has
been freed
Something we can have too much of or too little
of
In the moment but all of it we have is from
above
We try to put a price on it, creating an hourly
wage-
A part of the work structure and culture until we
reach a certain age.
We make choices in how we spend our "free"
time-
So many options, a lot we can do when we are in
our prime
Responsibilities and priorities place a limit
On how much of our "free" time we can use
down to the minute

It becomes a form of currency
To save up to use for another time or for an
emergency

We are given a fixed amount to be used as we
pleased
But it is close to empty-when we start running
out-we try harder to squeeze
More out to make up for the time we wasted.
Rarely, sometimes it can be created
When you take it away from something else
But it is still the same amount, just shuffled
about and rearranged
Simply an illusion-nothing really has changed.
It is how we spent it that will show what we
value
It can say a lot about us and what we most value.

Adulthood

Making choices-deciding on tasks
Deep down we do not want to do
There are consequences for the actions we do or
do not take
It is about making a decision and following
through

To tidy up the house to make it look pleasure
and clean
Or to allow dust to blanket every surface
And for the table to be covered in unread mail
and magazines?
To vacuum the floor to remove the crumbs
or to hang a sign around the cleaner saying "Out
of Service"?

To pay the bills on time when possible
Or to ignore them until the internet and electric
disappears or the water is shut off?
To plan and prepare your meals ahead
Or to order out on a daily basis and spend a lot
of money?
To make a budget and to stay within the
boundaries

Or to just burn through your money until you
have nothing left?

More choices can be presented until the nail
pierces through the board
Adulthood is about responsibility and making
the tough choice
It is said that the tough choice is the right one,
but we learn that down the road
Adulthood is about constantly learning from
your mistakes.

Quarter Life

Twenty five is the new fifty
Mid-life crisis but at an earlier time
Not enough time to be wise but enough to be
risky
Because they are still in their prime.

In college, what you learned in high school was
wrong
Being retaught, you become zealous to educate
the world
Once you get outside the sanctuary, the real
world hits you like a gong
You then wondered what went wrong

College taught me this, but the real world does
not operate that way
Due to the student debt, you need to find a job
that pays
It may go against what you believed during your
college days
But the quarter life crisis is just another phase.

Monday Morning

A weekend well spent-
Not knowing where the time went.
We never have enough
When Monday morning comes around

We do not want to go back to work
We have to give ourselves a pep talk in order to
get out of bed
A pot of coffee brewed the night before-
something planned ahead
The morning after the weekend may require
some teamwork

The kids do not want to go back to school
Forgot about the project or homework that was
due
They had a great time with their friends or at
their sporting event
But when Monday morning comes about, they
experience a feeling disorient.

We all make our way to work or to school
Doing our best to remember to get have some
morning fuel.

When Friday comes around, it will be a similar
routine
Different obligations and destinations like going
to the store to buy coffee beans.

But we are glad when there is more
The long weekend-3 days-Saturday, Sunday, and
Monday
But Tuesday becomes the new Monday but at
least the week is short-
Only four days instead of five to the weekend

To Do List

A catalog of endless tasks
A new one adding on the last
A hydra in paper form-when one is done; two
more take its place
Endless and cannot be outpaced

Once it is done, overflow of relief
Rains down over you, lasting either long or brief
A sense of accomplishment
Has no need of external acknowledgement

A day or two later, it comes back again
The hundred handed one returns to be sustained
It can start on small and grows over time
With tasks repeating almost actually as before or
having to them a similar rhyme

It just keeps going on and on
Like running a long marathon
But once it is done, overflow of relief
Rains down over you, lasting for a time long or
brief

Modern Riddles or Random Thoughts

If you do not take a picture of your workout,
Did you really go to the gym?

If you do not take a picture of the meal you
preferred at home,
Did you really cook?
Why healthy food does not have a great taste at
first
But the food that is not good for us tastes great?

We waste time on our phones, but we say we
save time.
Can both be true?
We spend so much time
Trying to manage our time
Only to waste more time.
Sounds like a hard cycle to break

We always want to reinvent the wheel
To make it better and to keep up with the spirit
of the age
But what about the old ways?
When will the new ways become the old way?

Surrounding Noise

With your eyes closed-What do you hear?

Outside:
Birds and crickets chirping
Traffic moving in the distance
Tires screeching on the road
Church bells ringing at the chapel down the road
The wind blowing through the cornfield

Inside:
A door in another room being opened
A TV show telling a story to its viewer
Ticking of the clock
The dog causing mischief
Water running into the sink
Pans clanging around while being moved
A light bulb going from dark to bright
The door closing behind someone who is leaving
the house